Black Sisters
Coloring Book

Aryla Publishing 2021

978-1-912675-98-2

www.arylapublishing.com

Stay Positive

Thank you for purchasing this book.

If you would like to know more about Aryla Publishing Books please visit:-

www.ArylaPublishing.com

Or follow us on
Facebook
Twitter
Instagram
for *free promotions*

@arylapublishing

We would love to know what you think of this book so please leave us a review.

Have a wonderful day ☺

Other Coloring Books from Aryla Publishing

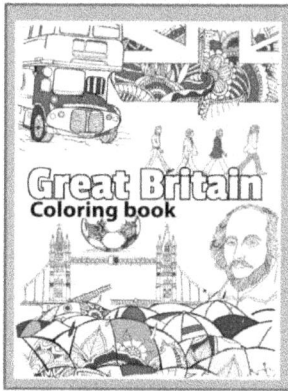

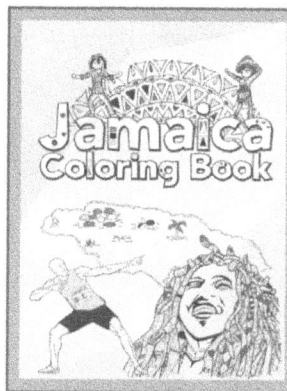

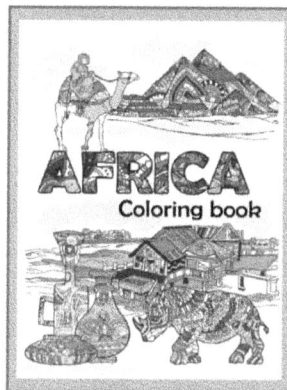

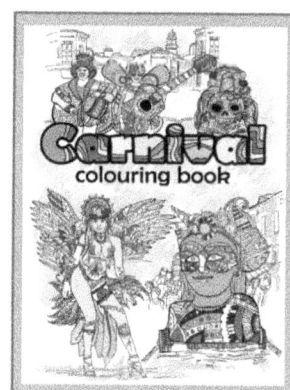

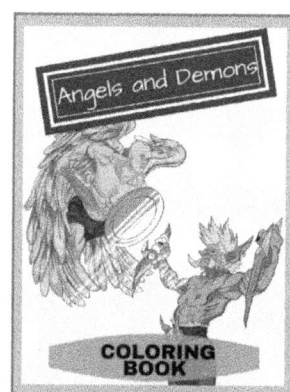

Great Britain Coloring book

U.S.A. Coloring book

Jamaica Coloring Book

Mexico Coloring book

PIRATE Coloring Book

Aryla Publishing

DRAGON Coloring Book

UNICORN Coloring Book

MERMAIDS Coloring Book

Black Inventors Coloring Book

Spain Coloring book

AFRICA Coloring book

Carnival colouring book

1920'S COLORING BOOK

Kittens and Puppies COLORING BOOK

Black Brothers COLORING BOOK

Angels and Demons COLORING BOOK

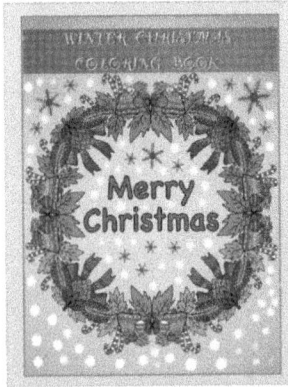

WINTER CHRISTMAS
COLORING BOOK

Merry
Christmas

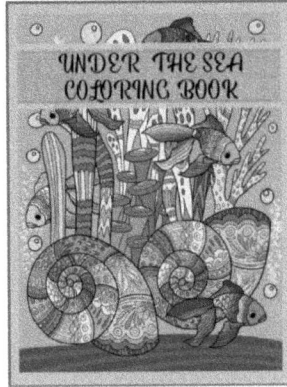

UNDER THE SEA
COLORING BOOK

CHRISTMAS
COLORING BOOK

Spain
Coloring book

HALLOWEEN
COLORING
BOOK

MOTHERS
DAY

Fathers Day
Coloring
Book

HALLOWEEN²
Coloring Book

SAME LOVE
Coloring Book

Valentine's day
COLORING
BOOK

EASTER
COLOURING
BOOK

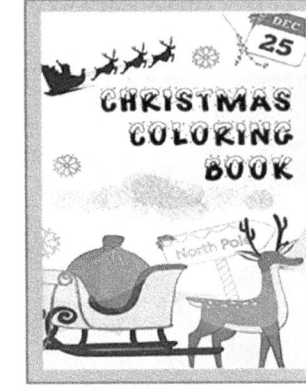

CHRISTMAS
COLORING
BOOK

North Pole

LOVE COLORING BOOK

HEALTH SERVICE

COLORING BOOK

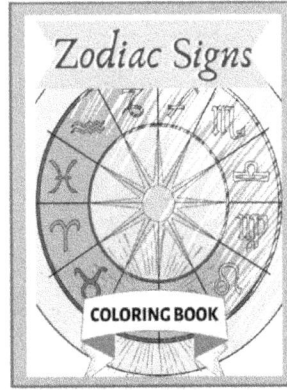

Zodiac Signs

COLORING BOOK

SPRING TIME
COLORING BOOK

JAPAN

FRANCE
Coloring Book

GREEK MYTHOLOGY

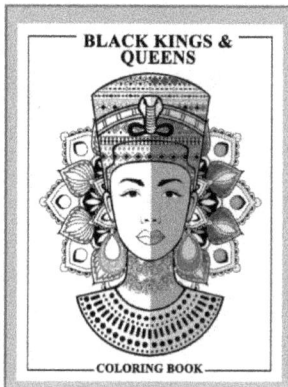
BLACK KINGS & QUEENS
COLORING BOOK

BLACK HEROES
Coloring Book

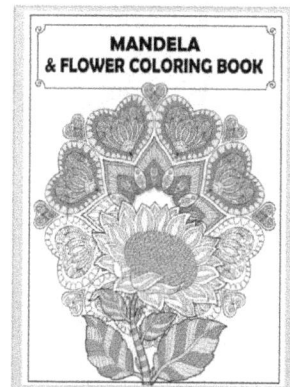
MANDELA & FLOWER COLORING BOOK

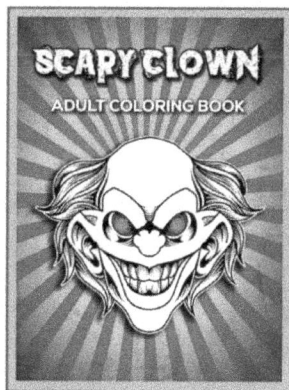
SCARY CLOWN
ADULT COLORING BOOK

CIRCUS
COLORING BOOK

ANIMAL COLORING BOOK

MYTHICAL CREATURES
Coloring Book

OWL
Coloring Book

TAROT COLORING BOOK

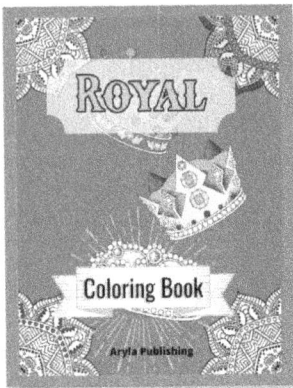
ROYAL
Coloring Book
Aryla Publishing

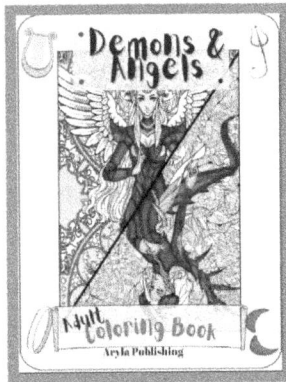
Demons & Angels
Adult Coloring Book
Aryla Publishing

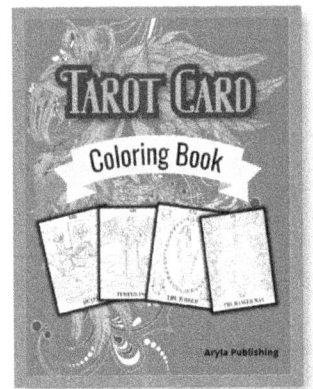
TAROT CARD
Coloring Book
Aryla Publishing

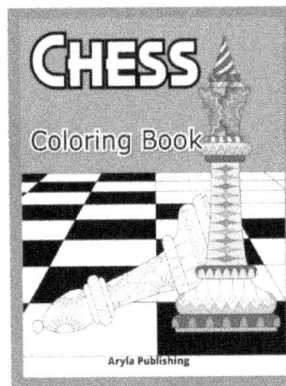
CHESS
Coloring Book
Aryla Publishing

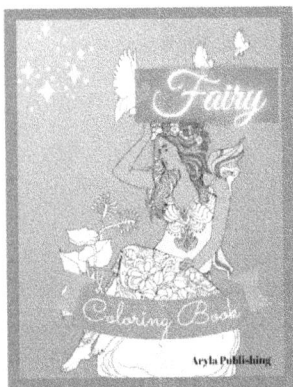
Fairy
Coloring Book
Aryla Publishing

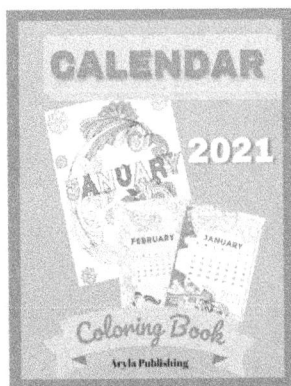
CALENDAR
2021
JANUARY
FEBRUARY JANUARY
Coloring Book
Aryla Publishing

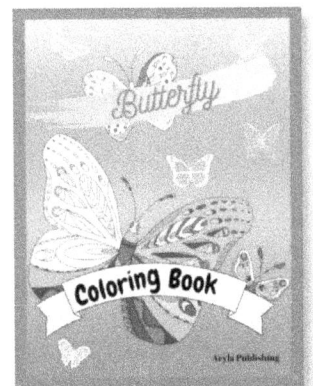
Butterfly
Coloring Book
Aryla Publishing

Color In Fun
Kids Books

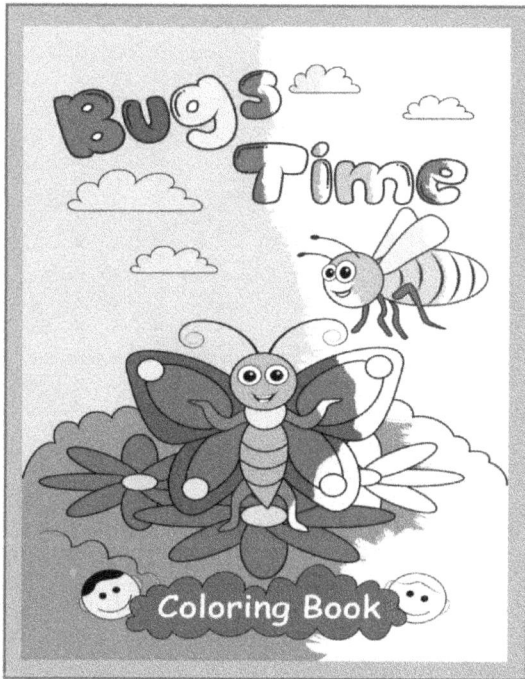

Bugs Time — Coloring Book

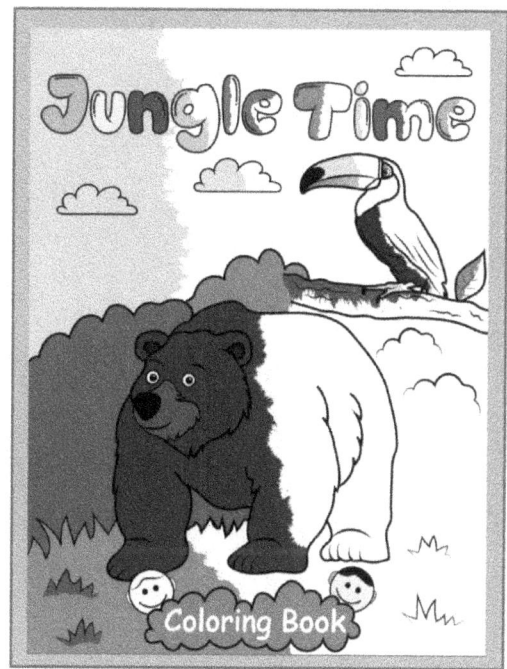

Jungle Time — Coloring Book

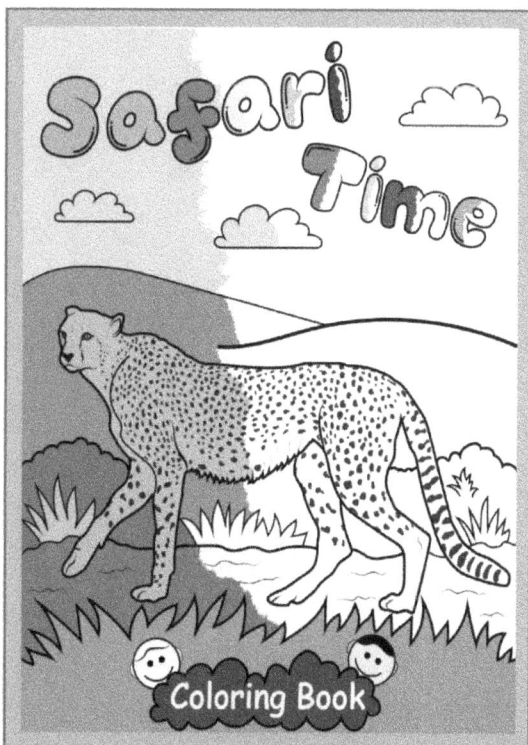

Safari Time — Coloring Book

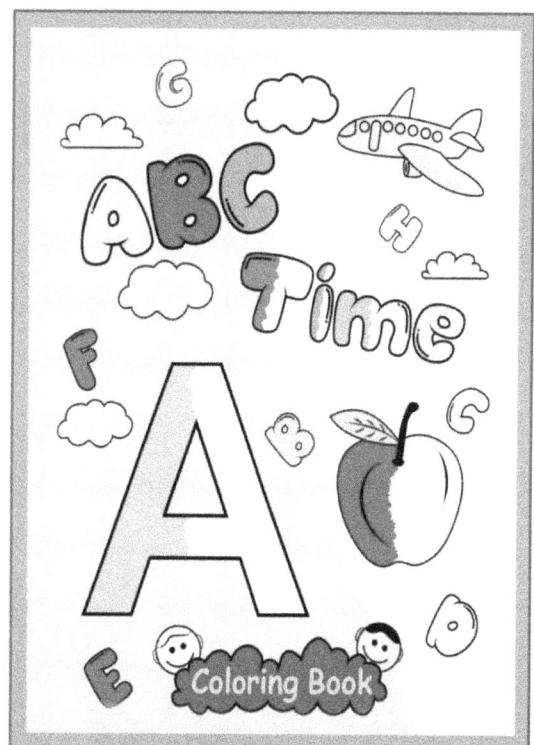

ABC Time — Coloring Book

Visit **www.ArylaPublishing.com**
to find out about all new releases.

Follow us @arylapublishing on Twitter Instagram & Facebook

Search for Aryla Publishing on

YouTube

Check out our Book Trailers

Subscribe to keep up to date with new releases!

WE WOULD LOVE YOUR FEEDBACK

PLEASE LEAVE REVIEW AT:-

www.ingramcontent.com/pod-product-compliance
Lightning Source LLC
Chambersburg PA
CBHW081723270326
41933CB00017B/3275